Discover India
State by State

OFF TO MADHYA PRADESH

SONIA MEHTA

PUFFIN BOOKS
An imprint of Penguin Random House

PUFFIN BOOKS

USA | Canada | UK | Ireland | Australia | New Zealand | India | South Africa | China | Singapore

Puffin Books is part of the Penguin Random House group of companies whose addresses can be found at global.penguinrandomhouse.com

Published by Penguin Random House India Pvt. Ltd
4th Floor, Capital Tower 1, MG Road,
Gurugram 122 002, Haryana, India

Penguin
Random House
India

First published in Puffin Books by Penguin Random House India 2017

Picture Credits

P 7: Fog at Orchha Railway Station, Madhya Pradesh (Elena Mirage/Shutterstock.com); P 9: Bamboo forest, Khajuraho, Madhya Pradesh (bodom/Shutterstock.com); P 12: Ujjain (AJP/Shutterstock.com), Jabalpur Railway Junction (bodom/Shutterstock.com); P 22: Maheswar, Madhya Pradesh (CRS PHOTO/Shutterstock.com); P 26: Devotees taking a dip during the Kumbha Mela (AJP/Shutterstock.com); P 28: Village houses (CRS PHOTO/Shutterstock.com); P 29: A village house (CRS PHOTO/Shutterstock.com); P 33: Bhimbetka caves (© Vijay Tiwari09 (Own work) [CC BY-SA 4.0 (http://creativecommons.org/licenses/by-sa/4.0)], via Wikimedia Commons); P 35: Tomb of Hoshang Shah (bodom/Shutterstock.com); P 38: Lal Bagh Palace (bodom/Shutterstock.com); P 39: Kharbuja Mahal (© Indrajit Das (Own work) [CC BY-SA 4.0 (http://creativecommons.org/licenses/by-sa/4.0)], via Wikimedia Commons); P 40: Farmers working on a field (B.Stefanov/Shutterstock.com); P 41: Workers at a factory (bodom/Shutterstock.com); P 43: An Indian blacksmith in Khajuraho (Aleksandar Todorovic/Shutterstock.com)

The views and opinions expressed in this book are the author's own and the facts are as reported by her, which have been verified to the extent possible, and the publishers are not in any way liable for the same.

The information in this book is based on research from bona fide sites and published books and is true to the best of the author's knowledge at the time of going to print. The author is not responsible for any further changes or developments occurring post the publication of this book. This series is not a comprehensive representation of the states of India but is intended to give children a flavour of the lifestyles and cultures of different states. All illustrations are artistic representations only.

ISBN 9780143440819

Design and layout by Quadrum Solutions Pvt. Ltd

Printed at Repro India Limited

www.penguin.co.in

This is a legitimate digitally printed version of the book and therefore might not
have certain extra finishing on the cover.

Hello Kids!

I'm so happy you are reading this book. India is an incredible country and there are lots of things about it that we never get to hear about.

I discovered India because my father was in the Indian army. He was posted to many places all over India—and we dutifully followed him. Can you imagine that by the time I was in the tenth standard, I had changed nine schools? Of course it was hard making new friends almost every year, but the good part was that I got to live in so many places. Right from Kerala, where I was born, to Kashmir, Jhansi, Shillong, Chandigarh, Goa . . . the list is long.

Every time I go to a new place, I feel amazed at how different each state is from the other—and yet, how similar. Did you know that we can see monuments from the Stone Age right here in India? Or that we have more than twenty official languages, and most Indians know three or four on an average? Or even that some of the world's most amazing scientific marvels were invented in India?

Oh, there are many, many, many fun and fantastic things about the states of India, which we simply must get to know.

So get your backpack ready, get set to meet some new friends and join me on a fun trip as we **DISCOVER INDIA, STATE BY STATE**.

I hope you enjoy reading this book as much as I have enjoyed writing it. I would love to hear from you. So do write to me at sonia.mehta@quadrumltd.com.

Lots of love,
Sonia Aunty

Mishki and Pushka have come to visit Earth from their home planet, Zoomba. They have never seen such an amazing place. Zoomba doesn't have trees and mountains and rivers like Earth does. But the people look exactly the same. When they come to Earth, they meet a sweet old man whom they call Daadu Dolma. Daadu Dolma shows them all the wonderful places in India and tells Mishki and Pushka all about them.

Mishki and Pushka can't believe what they see. They have seen a lot of Earth, but they have never, ever seen a place like India.

They are off to explore India state by state :)

Mishki

Mishki is a curious little girl. She is always asking loads of questions. On her home planet, she is always getting into trouble for poking her nose into things that are not her business.

Pushka is Mishki's brother.
He loves adventure. He is always ready
for a new challenge. Whether
it's climbing a mountain, or diving
into a cold, cold sea,
he is up for it.

Daadu Dolma

Daadu Dolma is a wise
old man who has lived on Earth longer
than the mountains and the seas. No one
knows quite how old he is, but
he certainly has been around.
He knows everything
about everything.

Mishki hasn't slept all night. She has been packing her bag for an exciting trip they are about to take.

'Daadu,' she says, 'what should we be packing for this trip?'

'Pack your binoculars, for sure,' says Daadu. 'We are going to see a lot of wildlife.'

'And will we get to eat some nice food?' pipes up Pushka, who is always hungry.

'Pushka, in no state of India will you ever be left hungry,' laughs Daadu. 'Here too you will taste some wonderful food, meet some truly great people and have a memorable time. Are you ready to leave?'

'YES!' chime Mishki and Pushka together. They are

OFF TO MADHYA PRADESH!!!

Land ahoy!

Daadu, I can't see any sea here. Isn't there any beach in this place?

No, Pushka. There is no sea near Madhya Pradesh. We are right in the middle of India. In fact, *madhya* means centre. So the meaning of Madhya Pradesh is the state in the centre.

Did you know?

At one time, Chhattisgarh was part of Madhya Pradesh.

A NICE NEIGHBOURHOOD

Madhya Pradesh has five friendly neighbours: Maharashtra, Uttar Pradesh, Chhattisgarh, Gujarat and Rajasthan form a ring around the state.

HILLS AND PLAINS

Madhya Pradesh has what you could call an easy and comfortable terrain. It is a part of the vast Indo-Gangetic Plains. There are gentle hills, lots of fertile plains and some plateaus too! The Vindhyas, the Kaimur Hills, the Maikala, the Mahadeo and the Satpura ranges all create peaks and valleys in the state.

ON THE MAP

To see exactly where Madhya Pradesh is on the map of India, go to

http://www.mapsofindia.com/maps/india/india-political-map.htm

PRIME PLATEAUS

There are three flat plateaus in Madhya Pradesh called the Malwa Plateau, the Bundelkhand Plateau and the Baghelkhand Plateau.

A BIT HOT, A BIT COLD, PLENTY WET

Monsoon weather patterns play games here. During summer, hot winds blow. Winters are cool enough for a shawl or a sweater. And the rains, on which the farmers depend so heavily, come pouring and water the many fields from June through September. The north of the state gets rain during December and January too!

RIVER RUSH

Some of India's most important rivers are born here and flow through this amazing state. The Narmada, Tapti, Mahanadi, Yamuna and Son are some. They meander through the state and make sure it gets plenty of water. Of course, they wait to get refilled during the rains, but having so many generous rivers does help the farmers a lot.

COLOURFUL SOIL

This state has rather colourful soil. Parts of Madhya Pradesh have black soil, which is very rich and fertile and perfect for farming. But parts of it even have red-to-yellow soil that isn't terribly fertile and farmers in this area have to struggle to make things grow.

CROP SHOP

Even though all of Madhya Pradesh doesn't have fertile soil, farming is still the largest occupation. Wheat, jowar, maize, rice, pulses—the brave farmers of Madhya Pradesh grow it all. They also grow sugarcane, cotton and different types of millet in the hilly regions.

WOW! The Narmada is so beautiful.

TREES APLENTY

There are some centuries-old trees in the forests of Madhya Pradesh that are very useful. Teak and sal have a hard wood that people use to build homes and furniture. Bamboo trees are useful for making a lot of articles. Salai is a tree that gives out a resin—something that is used to make medicines and incense.

You can make many things with bamboo.

Furniture made of teak wood

RIVER
WORD GRID

Can you find the names of the rivers that flow in Madhya Pradesh in this grid?

U	Y	N	R	E	W	Y	Q
U	Y	A	M	U	N	A	S
J	D	K	F	G	H	M	O
A	S	B	X	C	J	U	N
S	N	A	R	M	A	D	A
Z	A	D	S	V	W	A	N
Q	T	A	P	T	I	B	M
M	A	H	A	N	A	D	I

FOREST FABLES

It is said that at one time nearly one-third of the state was covered with forests. But that has become less with people cutting trees to increase farmland. The remaining hills have thick forests which are filled with wildlife.

Beautiful forests in the Bandhavgarh National Park

People say that Mowgli, Rudyard Kipling's much-loved wolf-boy in *The Jungle Book*, was actually the story of a little boy who lived with the wolves in a jungle in Pench in Madhya Pradesh.

How cool!

WILD AND WONDERFUL

You will get to see some amazing wildlife in this state because it has so many lush forests. There are many large mammals that roam these forests. Panthers, bears, tigers, deer and the rare barasingha are some. There are river dolphins and crocodiles in the rivers and swamps. Of course, there are many rare birds flitting around too!

A tiger at the Bandhavgarh National Park

KEEPING THEM SAFE

The government has realized that many animals are endangered. This is why they have set up many wildlife sanctuaries. The Kanha National Park, the Bandhavgarh National Park and the Shivpuri National Park are some where these magnificent animals can roam free and safe.

FUN FACTS

State animal
Barasingha

State flower
Palash

State bird
Dudhraj or paradise flycatcher

State tree
Banyan

Did you know?

The barasingha is called so because it has twelve tines (or branches to its antlers). Bara means twelve in Hindi.

FOREST MAZE

Mishki and Pushka are lost in the forest. They need to get to Daadu really fast. Which route should they take?

CITY CITY BANG BANG

BHOPAL

This is the capital city of Madhya Pradesh. It was once a princely state ruled by kings called nawabs. Now it's an important, modern city full of offices and factories.

INDORE

This city was first founded as a market town for traders to come and do business. It got its name from the Indreshwar Temple that was built by the local people.

UJJAIN

This is a very historical city that was once the capital of Emperor Ashoka's kingdom. Now it is an important centre for trade. The Kumbh Mela is also held here once every twelve years.

JABALPUR

This city used to be the headquarters of the Marathas, when they ruled this region. Now it is one of the state's most populated cities, and is an important railway junction.

KHAJURAHO

This incredible city is really ancient and is world famous for its wonderful sculptured temples. It draws tourists from across the world.

GWALIOR

The name of this city comes from a wonderful old rock fortress right at its centre. It's been called Gopa Parvat, Gopagiri and Gopadiri—all of which mean cowherd's hill. *Gwala* also means cowherd in Hindi.

HIDDEN WORDS

Look at the word. Such a big one! Can you make smaller words from it? Mishki has made one.

BARASINGHA

RING

Long, long ago

Daadu, what are those drawings on the wall?

They are cave paintings from ancient times, which were found in Madhya Pradesh. They tell us how old this state is and how people lived thousands of years ago.

AGES AGO

Heritage site of Bhimbetka in the east of Bhopal

Many rock paintings and stone and metal tools have been found in Madhya Pradesh. They tell us that people have lived in this region for millions of years. In recorded history, one of the first kingdoms we know about is the Avanti Kingdom. Under the rule of King Pradyota the Fierce, Avanti became a strong force and was one of the four most powerful kingdoms of North India.

Chandragupta Maurya

THE MIGHTY MAURYAS

Chandragupta Maurya, who was ruling over another powerful region called Magadha, had his eyes on Avanti. He conquered it and added it to his kingdom. Ujjain remained an important city for many years under Chandragupta's rule. This region soon came to be known as Malwa.

FIGHT FOR MIGHT

Coins from the Satavahana period

Many different kings wanted a slice of the Madhya Pradesh pie. Over the centuries, many kings conquered, ruled, established dynasties and were eventually defeated by other kings, who started their own dynasties. The Shungas, the Satavahanas, the Shakas and the Nagas were all powerful dynasties who ruled and left their mark on Madhya Pradesh. The Guptas were a strong dynasty who held power for a long time. They played an important role in India's history.

Coins tell us so much about a place. About kings and queens, about life and the gods people worshipped in those days.

SPOT THE DIFFERENCE

Mishki and Pushka have drawn some cave paintings. Can you spot ten differences in the two pictures?

WHO'S THE STRONGEST OF THEM ALL

The Huns were a bloodthirsty clan who came charging into the region. They overcame the Gupta Empire and grabbed the Kalachuri kingdom that was in a small part of Madhya Pradesh. But the Huns did not last, and the north of India broke into small kingdoms. King Harshavardhana, who was very powerful, oversaw the region for a while until his death.

Huns were bloodthirsty warriors.

Akbar was one of the greatest Indian rulers.

THEY CAME AND WENT

Many more dynasties came and went. The Chandelas ruled for a while. They are ones who built the incredible temples of Khajuraho. The Gonds were a clan who ruled for some time. The Tomara Rajput kingdom of Gwalior and the Sultanate of Malwa were still other kingdoms that ruled this region at different times.

STRONG INVADERS

When kings from middle eastern countries began to invade, rulers like Sultan Iltutmish formed the Delhi Sultanate, taking under their control many smaller kingdoms. (The Sultanate of Malwa was formed when it broke away from the Delhi Sultanate.) But it was Emperor Akbar who managed to take this entire region and a large part of India under his rule. The Mughal Empire, formed by Akbar's grandfather, Babur, was very powerful. Akbar made it even bigger and stronger.

MARATHAS COME KNOCKING

Later, the Marathas, led by Shivaji Maharaj, became a mighty force. They came from the south and began knocking hard on the Mughal doors. They soon took control of a large part of Malwa. But they too soon lost power. Two smaller dynasties, called the Scindias and Holkars, established themselves in Gwalior and Indore.

The Scindia and the Holkar families still play an active role in politics, though they are not royalty any more.

Shivaji led the Marathas to great victories.

WHAT'S ODD?

There's one name that doesn't fit in each row. Can you circle it?

| SHUNGAS | SAKAS | NAGAS | ROMANS |

| SCINDIA | MARATHA | GREEK | HOLKAR |

| SHIVAJI | JULIUS CAESAR | AKBAR | BABUR |

BAND OF ROBBERS

There were large bands of fierce robbers called Pindaris, who were making the entire region very unsettled. These Pindaris were, at one time, a part of the Maratha army, but they were on a rampage of their own. They made the entire region weak and just right for anyone who was strong to gain control.

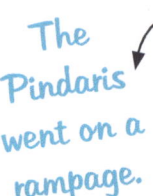

The Pindaris went on a rampage.

There were fierce fights among the British soldiers and the Indian people.

HERE COME THE BRITS

The British, who were slowly taking over India, found this region just perfect. They were easily able to overcome the Pindaris and a few weak dynasties that were struggling. They took control over the entire region. They were now ruling the entire country.

FIGHTING THE BRITISH

The Indians did not at all like the idea of being ruled by a foreign power. They preferred to solve their own problems. There were many struggles. Several people from Madhya Pradesh too fought in the rebellions. Finally, the British left India but not before dividing India into two countries—India and Pakistan.

M.P. IS BORN

When the British left India, it was divided into many smaller provinces. Parts of Maharashtra were included in the provinces that also had Madhya Pradesh. A few years after Independence, the government decided to reorganize the states. The Marathi-speaking part of Madhya Pradesh went to the state of Bombay (now Maharashtra). And many Hindi-speaking provinces were brought together and named Madhya Pradesh.

In some parts of Madhya Pradesh, people still speak Marathi fluently.

I want to learn both Hindi and Marathi.

MIXED-UP WORDS

Pushka is trying to remember the things he has learnt. Can you unscramble the words to help him out?

The Pindaris could be described as **ORBEBSR** _____.

Akbar was a **GALHUM** _____ emperor.

Madhya Pradesh became the state in which people spoke **IDNIH** _____.

Though Hindi is the official language here, it has many dialects. In the east and south, people speak Bagheli and Awadhi. In the north and centre, people speak a language called Bundeli or Bundelkhandi. In the west, people speak Malvi. Many tribes have their own dialects. Here are some words in Bundeli or Bundelkhandi.

I = Mein
Sit = Birajo
Walk = Chaliye
Eat = Khiye

How are you? = Tum kase aao?

What = Ka
What is your name? = Timao naam ka hai?

What is your favourite colour? = Tumao pasand ko rang kaun so hai?

I am fine = Hum theek ahi

What are you doing? = Tum ka karat ho?

LINGO SHINGO

Let's see how much you remember. Without looking at the words, match the English words to their Bundeli translations.

| I | Eat | What? | I am fine | How are you? | Sit | What are you doing? |

| Ka | Tum kase aao? | Mein | Khiye | Birajo | Tum ka karat ho? | Hum theek ahi |

A peep into their life

Daadu, is it time to sing some songs and dance? I'm waiting to learn new dances.

Yes, for sure. We can learn some lovely songs and do some fun dances because Madhya Pradesh has a really colourful culture. Time to explore!

TRIBAL TRAIL

Baiga tribes

There are many people in Madhya Pradesh who belong to really old tribes. Some of the most well-known are the Bhils, Gonds, Baigas, Kamars, Korkus and Marias. These colourful tribes have their own culture, their own unique way of celebrating festivals and their own music and dance too!

Though most of the people are Hindus, there are lots of Muslims, Christians, Jains and Buddhists as well!

EXCITING EPICS

Just like there is the Mahabharata and the Ramayana, the Gond tribes have their own epic stories called *Pandwani* and *Lachmanjati*. These epics also have songs and stories about gods and demons.

FOLKLORE FUN

Many tribes have very old songs and stories they pass on to their children down the generations. Pardhan are singers of the Gond tribe. They sing songs about a man called Lingo-Pen. They believe he was the man who began the Gond tribe.

There are folk musicians whose entire families are singers.

MATKI MAGIC

The *matki* dance is a skilful one, where women balance pots on their heads and make all kinds of complex moves. The pots are called matkis. Women perform this dance to celebrate festivals and big occasions.

This is so cool! Even I want to try this.

BADHAI BOOM

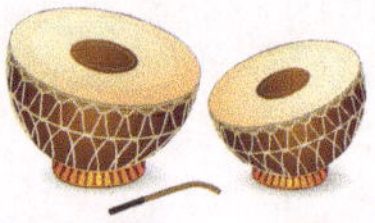

When there is a birth or a wedding in the family or even a festival, people get together to do this energetic dance. It is performed by men and women who wear colourful traditional costumes and perform intricate dance steps.

DADARIYA DELIGHT

During Dussehra, the men from one village visit other villages in search of brides. They are welcomed by young girls, who do the *dadariya* dance, after which they choose their own groom.

JAUNTY JAWARA

People do this dance to celebrate a good harvest. Women carry baskets of grain on their heads. Men join in and dance to the beat of drums, cymbals and bells. It's great fun to watch and even greater fun to do.

What a fun dance this is!

A good harvest is a big reason to celebrate!

TERRIFIC TERTALI

This wonderful dance is mainly performed by people of the Kamar tribe. It's a skilful dance, all right. Women squat on the ground. There are cymbals and bells tied to parts of their body that make musical sounds when they move. During the more complex moves, they carry a lot of weight on their heads and swords clenched in their teeth. Whoa! Careful!

EXCITING EVENTS

There are lots of events like festivals, fairs and religious gatherings that people participate in with gusto in Madhya Pradesh. Come, let's visit some.

SIMHASTA MELA

This is the local name for the Kumbh Mela. This enormous gathering of people from across the world is held once every twelve years at Ujjain. They take a dip in the holy waters, pray at the *Shiv Ling* and meditate.

IJTIMA AT BHOPAL

This Islamic event, which is held in Bhopal every year, is among the world's largest religious gatherings. The devotees are called *Jamatees*. They come from places across the world, like Russia, Kazakhstan, France, Indonesia, Malaysia, Africa and many others too. Sermons and prayers are held through the days and nights at this three-day festival. There is also a colourful fair that goes on side by side.

TANSEN MUSIC FESTIVAL

Tansen was a great musician in the court of Akbar. They say that when he sang, the heavens would open up and pour down on everyone, such was the power of his voice. Though he lived hundreds of years ago, people still honour him. He is buried in Gwalior, and a four-day music festival is held there every year.

BHAGORIA HAAT FESTIVAL

This is a festival that is lots of fun. *Bhag* means to run. During this festival, which is just a little before Holi, the boys put *gulal* (red powder) on the face of the girl they want to marry. If she too wants to marry him, she puts the same colour on his face. Then they both run away, as fast as they can, from that spot. All this is done with a lot of dancing, singing and merriment.

Sounds fun, especially if you do want to get married, right?

MATCH THEM RIGHT

Mishki is trying to recall the details of each festival. Help her by matching the words that go with each festival.

BHAGORIA •   • One of the world's largest religious gatherings

TANSEN •   • Carrying a sword between the teeth

IJTIMA •   • Carrying a basket of grain on their head

TERTALI •   • Put gulal and run

JAWARA •   • A grand musical festival

Bricks and Stones

Madhya Pradesh looks really interesting. Can we actually go inside some houses and see how people live?

Sure, Mishki. As long as we don't disturb them. Come, let me tell you the different kinds of homes people here have.

TINY VILLAGE HOUSES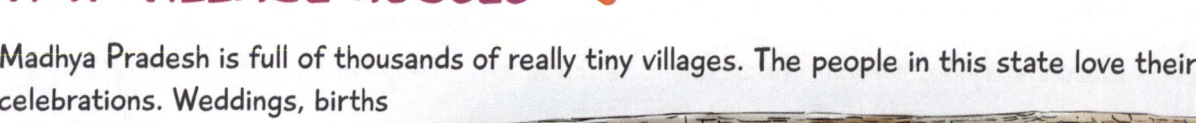

Madhya Pradesh is full of thousands of really tiny villages. The people in this state love their celebrations. Weddings, births or festivals—they sing, dance and enjoy every moment. That is why you will find their houses are built so that all these functions can be held in the house itself.

The Saharia tribe builds houses in a circular arrangement.

The Bhils build their houses in a scattered pattern.

The Korku tribe builds houses in neat lines.

LIVING TOGETHER

The villages in this state are tiny. The villagers like to have plenty of neighbours, so that they can drop into each other's homes and spend time together. That is why even when they build houses, they build them close to each other. Some build their houses in tight circles, some in neat lines and some are scattered with no pattern—but close to their neighbours.

Many village houses are built with simple mud walls and thatched roofs made of bamboo hay.

SPENDING TIME TOGETHER

Because people like to pray, sing and dance together, the houses always have a large common courtyard. Here, the older people sit and chat, while keeping an eye on grandchildren, since usually both parents work in the fields. Family members also collect here and do all their domestic work, like drying chillies and sunning pickles.

A chaupal is a public space in a village, where the villagers gather to discuss their problems, sort out disputes and celebrate festivals. It is a raised platform around a big, shady banyan tree. The elders of the village meet here and spend time discussing the matters concerning the village.

HOUSES WITH OCCUPATIONS

Many houses are designed based on what the main occupation of a family is. There are farmers, potters, bamboo workers, weavers—all of whom design their homes to suit their occupations. Let's see a few homes.

A POTTER'S HOME

In a potter's house, there is lots of space for raw materials as well as pots. Sometimes there is a yard in the front for selling pots right from home. Often, there is a shed for a donkey, the family pet, who helps carry pots to the marketplace to sell.

HOUSE OF BAMBOO

There are many, many craftsmen who make things using bamboo. These people live near the forests, so they can easily cut and carry bamboo home to work on. The walls are made of bamboo—naturally—and then covered thickly with mud. The doors, windows and roof are all made using parts of bamboo. These people also keep a part of their house to store their baskets, mats and other things they craft with bamboo.

NICE AND BRIGHT

The one thing that all the people of Madhya Pradesh have in common is their love for colour and pattern. Village houses are almost always decorated with lovely paintings and patterns. But these are not only decorative. They have a meaning too! There are animals, human figures, birds, flowers and trees—all of which are symbols of what the people believe in. There are also designs on the floor that women create to celebrate festivals.

Some villagers paint their walls in brilliant colours of blue and pink. Looks cheerful, doesn't it?

PAINTING PRETTY

Look at this beautiful Gond art. Can you draw it yourself? Mishki is longing to.

Draw here

Standing strong

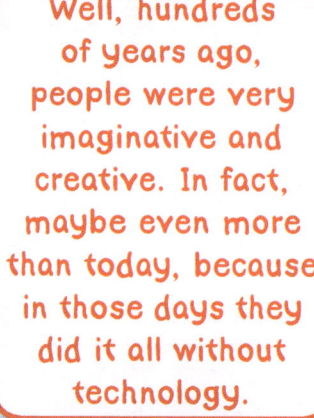

Well, hundreds of years ago, people were very imaginative and creative. In fact, maybe even more than today, because in those days they did it all without technology.

Daadu, we have seen how people live today. But what about hundreds of years ago? What kind of buildings did they build those days?

THE MAGIC OF KHAJURAHO

The temples of Khajuraho are world famous and people come here by the millions to gaze at the wonderful sculptures and carvings done so many centuries ago. Built by kings of the Chandela dynasty, the sculptures on the temple walls give us a glimpse into the lifestyle of people back then. At one time, there were more than eighty temples, but many of them have fallen to ruin. The government has stepped in to preserve these and you can see more than twenty temples and marvel at the skill of the sculptors.

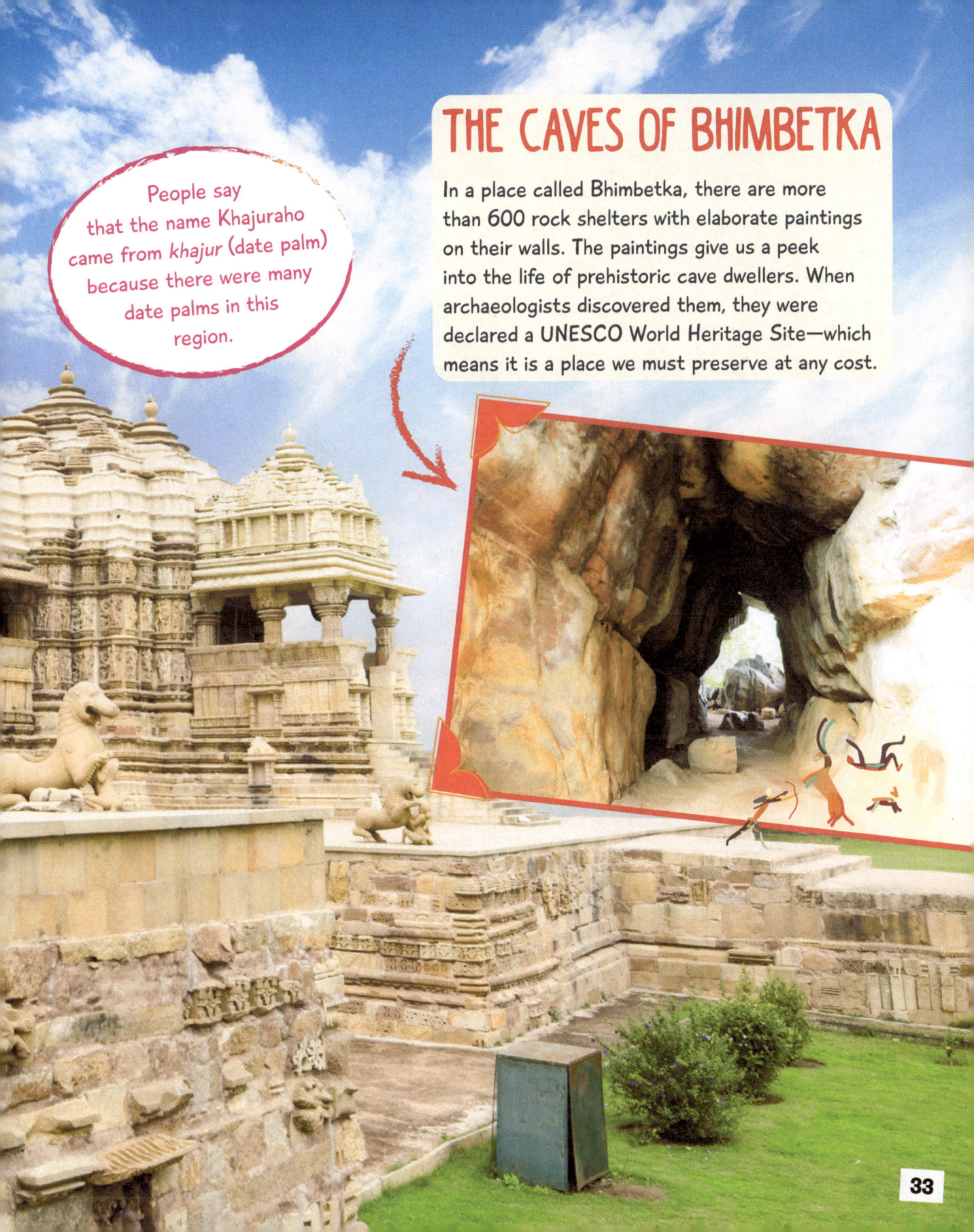

People say that the name Khajuraho came from *khajur* (date palm) because there were many date palms in this region.

THE CAVES OF BHIMBETKA

In a place called Bhimbetka, there are more than 600 rock shelters with elaborate paintings on their walls. The paintings give us a peek into the life of prehistoric cave dwellers. When archaeologists discovered them, they were declared a UNESCO World Heritage Site—which means it is a place we must preserve at any cost.

This is so beautiful.

SANCHI STUPA

When you visit the little town of Sanchi, you will feel as if you have gone right back to the time of King Ashoka the Great. King Ashoka was a devout Buddhist. He had seen so much bloodshed during the war he fought against Kalinga that he gave up war and decided to spread Buddha's message of peace instead. He built many, many monasteries, temples and stupas with Buddha's messages carved on them. The Sanchi Stupa is one such.

A stupa is a dome-like building that has holy importance for Buddhists.

MAGNIFICENT MANDU

This is an incredible historical city that has many spellbinding stories and legends hidden in its forts and palaces. Sadly, many of them are in ruins. But still, we can see its magnificence and creativity. Let's visit some of them.

THE SWINGING PALACE

Hindola Mahal means just that. This incredible palace in Mandu has slanting walls that make it look like it is swinging. It is so large that it actually has more palaces, buildings and lakes within it. It is believed that the Mughal kings used this palace to chill out in.

Roopmati Pavilion in Mandu

BAZ BAHADUR PALACE

This wonderful palace is a star attraction in Mandu. There are courtyards, grand arches, hundreds of rooms and verandas—all of which tell you how wonderful it must have been to be a king in those far off days. You have a lovely view of Rani Roopmati's Pavilion, and you can just imagine the king and his lovely queen strolling through the gardens.

Rani Roopmati

The love story of the gallant Sultan Baz Bahadur and his wife, the beautiful Rani Roopmati, is a legend that people love to hear. The story goes that when Akbar's army defeated her husband, she poisoned herself rather than become a prisoner of the enemy.

HOSHANG SHAH'S TOMB

People say that this is India's oldest marble tomb and even Emperor Shah Jahan, who built the Taj Mahal, was inspired by it. It has a vast dome and lots of detailed jali work, through which light filters in, making the place look magical.

JAHAZ MAHAL

This means 'the ship palace'. It's called that as it looks like it is floating on water. They say that Sultan Ghiyas-ud-din Khilji built it especially for his harem. (A harem is a group of women who entertained the king.)

FANTASTIC FORTS

With such a rich history of so many battles being fought, the forts of Madhya Pradesh have an important place in its history.

MAHESHWAR FORT

This fort was built by Ahilya Bai Holkar. Her people loved her so much that even now, hundreds of years after her death, the local people feel as if she is watching over them. The fort is now a hotel.

GWALIOR FORT

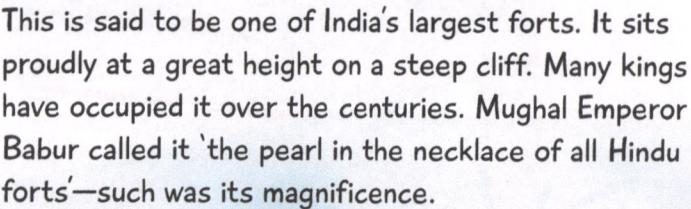

This is said to be one of India's largest forts. It sits proudly at a great height on a steep cliff. Many kings have occupied it over the centuries. Mughal Emperor Babur called it 'the pearl in the necklace of all Hindu forts'—such was its magnificence.

CHANDERI FORT

Chanderi is a town that is today known more for its weavers. But at one time, it was a town at the centre of a lot of battles and bloodshed. It was built by the Mughals many hundreds of years ago. Its main gate is called Khooni Darwaza—which means gateway of blood. Eeep! That sounds scary, all right. Imagine how brutal life must have been back then. As different kings ruled, they built temples, mosques and palaces inside.

THAT'S SCARY!

CROSSWORD TIME

Can you help Pushka solve this crossword? He is going crazy trying to figure it out.

ACROSS

1. The name of the famous Buddhist stupa in Mandu.

4. The king who built the famous stupa.

5. Roopmati's title in Hindi.

6. The world-famous carved temples.

10. The organization that declares a place a world heritage site.

11. The city that is full of wonderful palaces and temples.

DOWN

1. A Buddhist monument with a dome.

2. The palace that people feel swings.

3. A temple of meditation and worship for Buddhists.

7. The group of women who used to entertain kings.

8. The state of a temple that has fallen into disrepair.

9. A burial building.

PALACE PERFECT

Of course, there are many palaces here too! With so many kings and queen livings here, how could there not be? How about peeping into some of them?

THE LAL BAGH PALACE

This beautiful palace in Indore is less than 200 years old but is impressive, all right. Built by the Holkar family, it has a strong Western influence. It has a huge ballroom, Persian carpets, stained-glass windows and Italian-style paintings. And guess what! Its massive kitchens are on the other side of the river. A long underground tunnel goes below the river and into the main palace. Can you imagine how much people had to run around to get food to the table?

GOHAR MAHAL

Here's something interesting. For a long time, the princely state of Bhopal was under the rule of queens. One particular queen called Qudisiya was very smart and progressive. She was a great ruler and did a lot for people. She brought women out from behind the purdah (veil). She built Gohar Mahal, a beautiful palace in which she lived for many years.

KHARBUJA MAHAL

Kharbuja means melon. That explains the funny name because this lovely palace has domes that look just like melons. It's also a scientific wonder, because the rooms of this palace need no coolers or air conditioners. They are designed so that the warm air rises and escapes, making way for cool air to replace it. Though a lot of Mughals lived here in their time, the Peshwas lived here for a while too.

> Imagine a palace being inspired by a fruit. I'd love to see this one.

RHYME TIME

Mishki wants to make a poem about forts. She needs five words that rhyme with fort. Can you help her?

FORT

_____ _____ _____ _____ _____

Working hard

So, Daadu, I've been wondering. What kind of work do people actually do here? Are they all farmers?

No, Pushka. The largest number of people living here are farmers, but there are many other things people do for a living. Let's see what they are.

FARMER, FARMER, WHAT DO YOU GROW?

We have already seen how farming is the largest activity, thanks to the fertile plains in this state. Apart from rice, wheat and the main crops, farmers are busy cultivating soya beans, sugarcane and cotton too!

ANIMAL FARM

There are lots of farmers who rear cows, buffaloes, goats and sheep. In fact, a lot of India's livestock is reared in Madhya Pradesh. The many rivers and canals give fishermen a livelihood too!

FACTORY AND MILLS

Madhya Pradesh is a very busy state. There are many factories producing all kinds of things. Paper, cement, heavy electrical items, sugar, textiles—all these are just some of the things that are made here in factories on a large scale. These factories give employment to lots of people.

A paper mill in Madhya Pradesh

HAPPY FARM

Pushka wants to start a farm. He needs animals for it. Can you help him find the farm animals in this picture and circle them?

COOLEST CRAFT

Madhya Pradesh is home to some of India's most skilled craftsmen. For generations, men and women have been creating masterpieces in textiles, clay, metals and other materials. Let's meet some of these wonderful craftsmen and see what they do.

SARI MAGICIANS

Women go crazy about some of the beautiful weaves from this state. *Chanderi* and *Maheshwari* are just two types of sari fabrics that are made in brilliant colours. Women from all over the world buy these. There are many block printers who print wonderful patterns on cloth to make saris and other lovely prints.

Wow! Such minute detail!

WOOD WORKERS

The woodcraft of Madhya Pradesh is ever so famous. The wood workers make intricate wooden animals, human figures and other shapes. The tribal people living near forests have been doing this for generations and still make and sell these.

The woodcraft is magical!

BLACKSMITH GENIUS

The blacksmith's craft, that is, moulding iron into shapes, is nearly as old as the land itself. There are many blacksmiths, called *lohars*, who make wonderful iron objects, like diyas, knives, axes and ornaments. As people become more modern, these blacksmiths too are coming up with newer and more modern designs.

The metal needs to be red-hot so that it can be moulded into amazing shapes.

Perfect Print

Mishki is impressed with the block prints. She wants to make one too! Can you trace and redraw the same print that she has?

Draw here

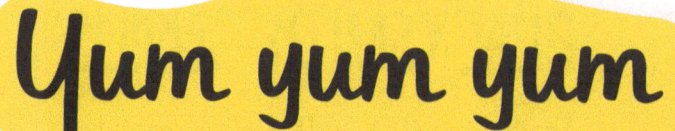

Yum yum yum

Can we eat something now, Daadu? All that travelling has made me terribly hungry.

You are always hungry, Pushka. But this time, I am too!

Well, then, what are we waiting for? We are going to taste the diverse and delicious food of Madhya Pradesh.

DIVERSE AND DELICIOUS

That just about describes food in this state. The different parts of the state have different styles of cooking—some of it similar to that of the neighbouring states. Bundelkhand, Mahalkhoshal, Malwa, Nimar—all these are different cuisines. But let's taste some of the most popular dishes.

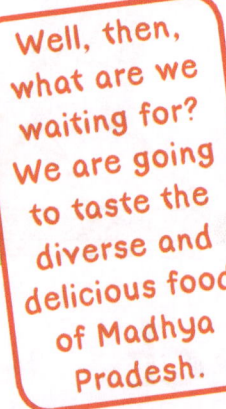

BHUTTE KI KEES

Imagine golden corn, grated and cooked with milk. This is a lovely street-food snack that the people of Indore love to eat.

DAAL BAFLA

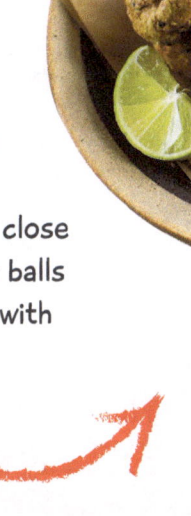

This scrumptious dish is similar to Rajasthan's daal baati—not surprising, considering they are such close neighbours. Golden wheat balls are dunked in dal and had with chutney. After which you can have a nice long nap.

CHAKKI KI SHAAK

This is another dish inspired by Rajasthani cuisine. The wheat dough is steamed and then cooked with a lot of spices. People love eating this with curd. It's a bit like its first cousin, gatte ki sabzi.

BHOPALI GOSHT KORMA

This meat dish makes you feel like you are at a Mughal feast. It has lots of fragrant spices and was cooked in the royal kitchens for nawabs. No wonder you feel royal when you eat it.

SWEET SOMETHINGS

The people from Madhya Pradesh have a very sweet tooth. Here are some yummy desserts you can't stay away from.

Yummmmy!

MEVA BATI

This sweet dish couldn't be sweeter. It's like the famous gulab jamun. Mava (reduced milk) balls are deep fried and then soaked in sugar syrup.

RAAS KHEER

There are many versions of this across North India. But this one from Bundelkhand is special. It's a pudding made from the mahua flower, milk and millet. And you know what? It's healthy too because you don't need to add sugar, that's how naturally sweet it is.

LAVANG LATIKA

This isn't the name of a girl. It's a yummy dish. It's made of little pockets of rolled-out wheat dough stuffed with coconut and dry fruits. The top is held closed by a clove (lavang), and then it's fried and soaked in sugar syrup. Nice name and nice taste too!

BHOPALI PAAN

It's time to end the feast with this popular paan that people across the country love. The betel leaf is stuffed with a unique mixture. Making the perfect paan is considered an art in Bhopal. But remember, it's only for grown ups. You might not like the taste too much, either.

MISHKI THE POET

Mishki is writing a poem for Pushka about food. She needs just three words that rhyme with food. Can you help her?

FOOD _____ _____ _____

What to wear?

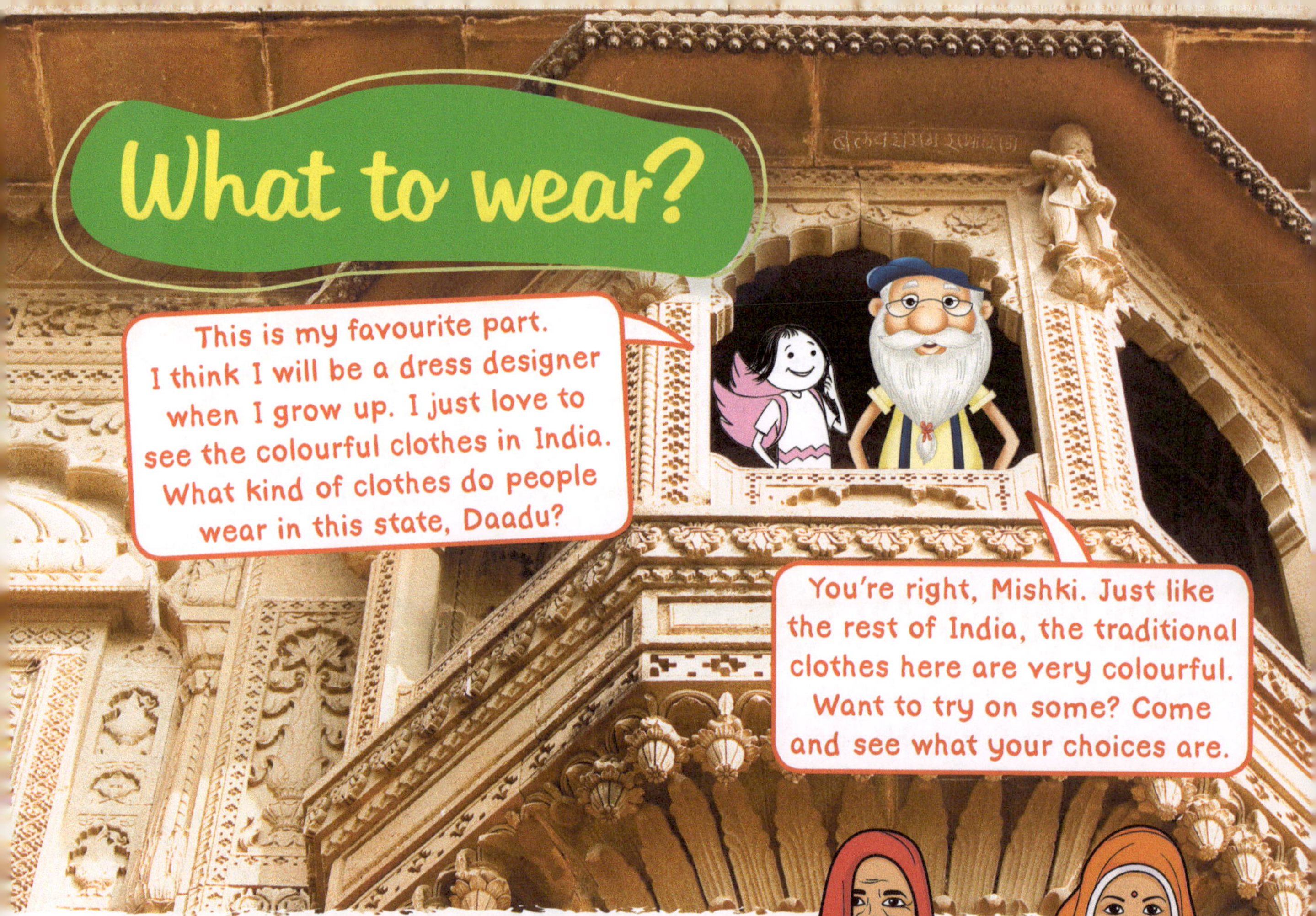

This is my favourite part. I think I will be a dress designer when I grow up. I just love to see the colourful clothes in India. What kind of clothes do people wear in this state, Daadu?

You're right, Mishki. Just like the rest of India, the traditional clothes here are very colourful. Want to try on some? Come and see what your choices are.

LET'S GO TRADITIONAL

Traditionally, women wore a lehnga (a long, wide skirt) and a choli (blouse). They would have a long colourful cloth called a *lugra* or *orni* that they would use to cover their shoulder and head. Their favourite colours were black and red. But now, even the more traditional women wear regular saris.

What amazing colours! Even modern women dress traditionally for festivals and occasions.

WHAT THE MEN WEAR

The traditional outfit for most men in Madhya Pradesh is a dhoti. Over a shirt or kurta, they add a jacket called a *mirzai* or *bandi*. And it's topped off with a turban called a *safa*. For celebrations and festivals, the men go colourful.

Tribal men wear a dhoti too, but it's much shorter than what city dwellers wear. It is also called a langot.

TRIBAL TREAT

The tribal women love chunky jewellery. They jingle around, wearing lots of necklaces, bangles, bracelets and *pyheb* (anklets). Women in some tribes wear a half sari. And some tribals wear a lot of unusual headgear, especially during festivals and weddings.

TERRIFIC TATTOOS

Many rural and tribal people decorate their arms and even faces with tattoos. These tattoos are not fashion statement. They have religious symbolism. Sometimes they even design the image of a god.

HIDDEN WORDS

How many words can you find hidden in the word given below. Pushka found ten.

HEADGEAR

HEAD _____   _____

_____   _____

_____   _____

Autograph, please?

Daadu, will we meet kings and queens?

Probably not, because we met them all in the history section. But there are many famous people who were born in this state and went on to become really famous in different parts of the world. Let's meet some of them.

ATAL BIHARI VAJPAYEE

He was a politician who went on to become the prime minister of India, not once but twice. He was the tenth prime minister of India. He was also awarded the Bharat Ratna, the highest award an Indian can receive.

Did you know?
Atal Bihari Vajpayee was the prime minister for thirteen days when he was elected for the first time.

CHANDRASHEKHAR AZAD

Born Chandrashekhar Tiwari, he got the title of *Azad* (meaning free) for his fierce fight for India's independence. He was a firebrand freedom fighter, who played an important role in India's freedom struggle.

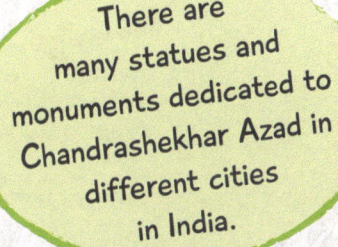

There are many statues and monuments dedicated to Chandrashekhar Azad in different cities in India.

VIJAYA RAJE SCINDIA

Married to the Maharaja of Gwalior, Vijaya Raje Scindia went on to do a lot for the people as Rajmata of Gwalior. She became an important politician and continued to work for the people.

MANSOOR ALI KHAN PATAUDI

People call him Tiger Pataudi.

Everyone knows this famous nawab from Bhopal who became a cricketer. He played many matches for India. His son, Saif Ali Khan, is a famous actor in Hindi movies.

TANTIYA BHEEL

He was called the Indian Robin Hood. He was a bandit who fought fiercely against the British. A lot of people think of him as a hero.

RATNESH PANDEY

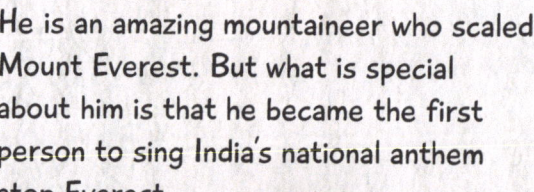

He is an amazing mountaineer who scaled Mount Everest. But what is special about him is that he became the first person to sing India's national anthem atop Everest.

KAILASH SATYARTHI

He was a great social reformer who fought against child labour and for the right to education for every child. He was awarded the Nobel Peace Prize in 2014, along with Malala Yousafzai.

MANNU BHANDARI

She is a famous author who has written many books. She started the 'Nayi Kahaani' movement, which urged authors to write about present-day issues.

HARISHANKAR PARSAI

Harishankar Parsai was a writer who wrote humorous stories in Hindi. He had a simple style that people loved.

ODD ONE OUT

Pushka wants to be a famous person. He can't decide what he should be. Help him decide by finding out which profession is odd from each row below. Circle it for him.

| DANCER | SINGER | POLITICIAN | PAINTER |

| CRICKETER | SWIMMER | ARTIST | FOOTBALLER |

| POET | WRITER | ACTOR | PLAYWRIGHT |

Once upon a time . . .

Oh yay! It's story time. I love listening to stories. What are you going to tell us today, Daadu?

THE FAIR DEAL

I am going to tell you a very popular story from Madhya Pradesh—and it is something you will learn from too. Many folk tales have a lesson hidden in them. Let me see if you can find the lesson hidden in this one.

There was a kingdom in Madhya Pradesh called Bhopal. It was a prosperous place and the people who lived there were all well off.

In this prosperous kingdom, there lived a rich merchant, who had three sons—Bansilal, Shyamlal and Ramlal. The merchant was as wise as he was rich. No wonder his business prospered.

One day, he thought to himself: *I am building this business. But who will look after it after I am gone?* He decided to test his three sons and decide who was the most worthy of them all—and who would be able to run the business in the same fair and honest way he had done.

He called his three sons to him and gave them a test.

'My sons, I am getting old. I would like to hand over my business to one of you. But first, I want to see who is the most worthy. So I want you to complete a task for me,' he said.

Ramlal and Shyamlal's eyes gleamed. They were greedy and in a rush to take over the business.

'Tell us what you want us to do,' they said eagerly.

'I want you to steal a coin for me, so stealthily that even God cannot see you do it,' the merchant said.

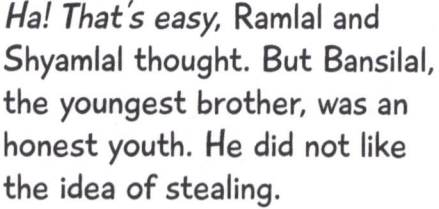

Ha! That's easy, Ramlal and Shyamlal thought. But Bansilal, the youngest brother, was an honest youth. He did not like the idea of stealing.

That night, Ramlal stole a coin from his father's safe. Shyamlal stole a coin from his mother's trunk. They handed over the coins to the merchant.

'No one saw us take the coins,' they assured him. 'We made sure there was no picture or idol of any god around.'

The merchant just looked at them. Then he asked Bansilal, 'Where is your coin, Bansi?'

Bansilal looked down. 'Stealing is wrong, Babuji. Also, God is everywhere. So how could I steal without Him knowing? He sees everything. That is what you have taught us.'

The merchant smiled. He was pleased with Bansilal's answer.

'Now for your next task,' he said to his three sons. 'Here is a one-rupee coin for each of you. Go and make a fair deal that will completely fill up this room with something.'

Ha! Easy, the older sons thought gleefully. They considered themselves fabulous businessmen already.
Off the three went to
fulfil this new task.

Ramlal went and bought an enormous sack of loose chaff. He took it home and spread it across the floor. But it was nowhere near enough to fill the room. He wanted to get more, but he had used up his coin. On his way out of the house, he saw a beggar, asking for alms. He shoved the beggar aside and stomped off angrily.

Shyamlal bought a huge sack of cotton, quite sure it would fill the room. But alas! It barely spread across the floor. He too stomped his way off. He met the beggar, and pushed him aside furiously.

Bansilal stepped out of the house, wondering what to do. He saw the poor beggar and felt so sorry for him that he gave him the coin.

Now he had nothing left to buy something with. So he went to the kitchen and found an old candle. He took the candle and a matchbox. He went into the room and lit the candle. At once, the entire room was filled with light.

The merchant was watching all this, for it was he who was dressed as a beggar. His heart filled with joy when he saw what Bansilal had done. He knew he had found his successor.

He left the entire business to Bansilal and the business grew and grew till Bansilal became one of the most rich and famous men in all of Madhya Pradesh.

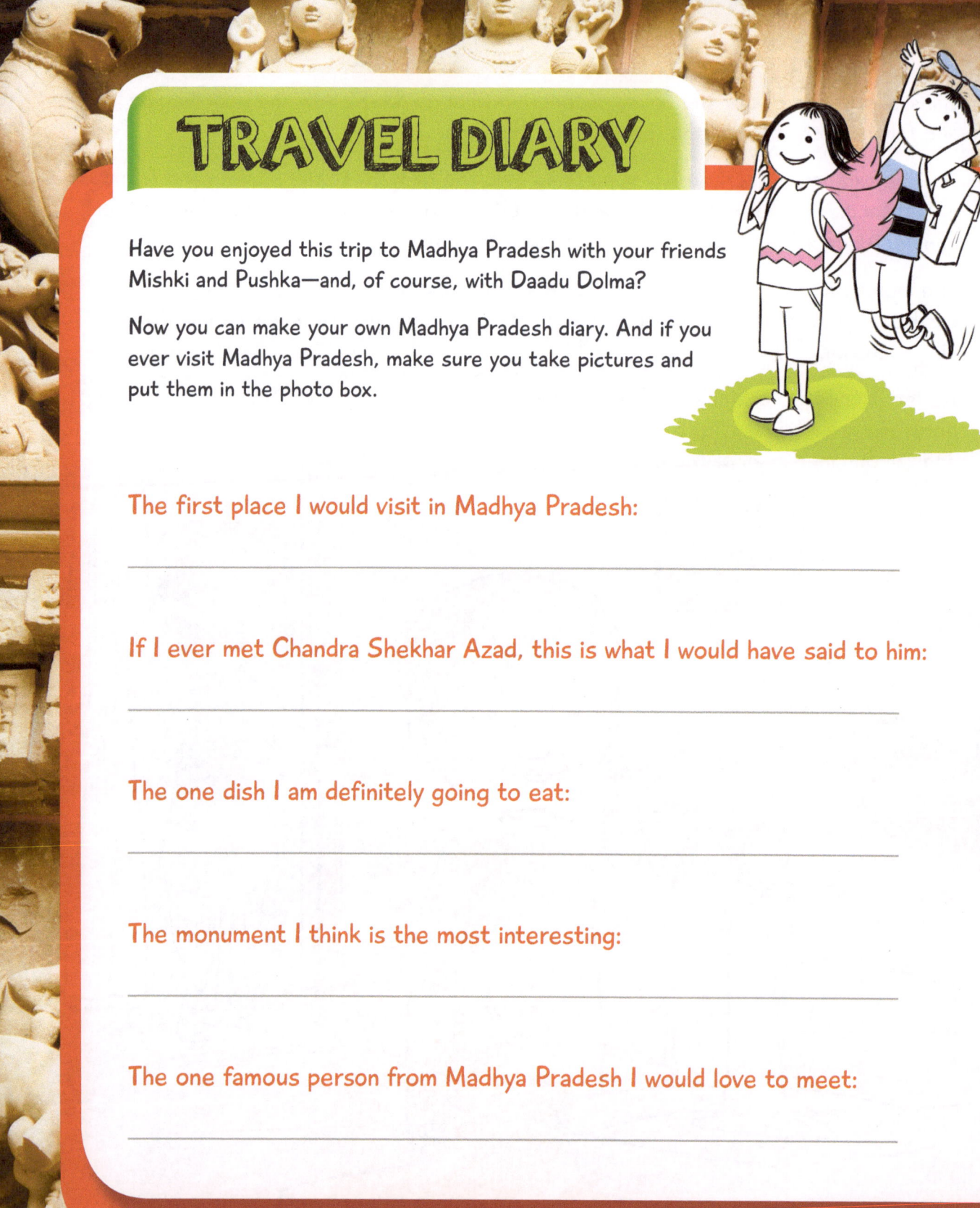

TRAVEL DIARY

Have you enjoyed this trip to Madhya Pradesh with your friends Mishki and Pushka—and, of course, with Daadu Dolma?

Now you can make your own Madhya Pradesh diary. And if you ever visit Madhya Pradesh, make sure you take pictures and put them in the photo box.

The first place I would visit in Madhya Pradesh:

_____

If I ever met Chandra Shekhar Azad, this is what I would have said to him:

_____

The one dish I am definitely going to eat:

_____

The monument I think is the most interesting:

_____

The one famous person from Madhya Pradesh I would love to meet:

_____

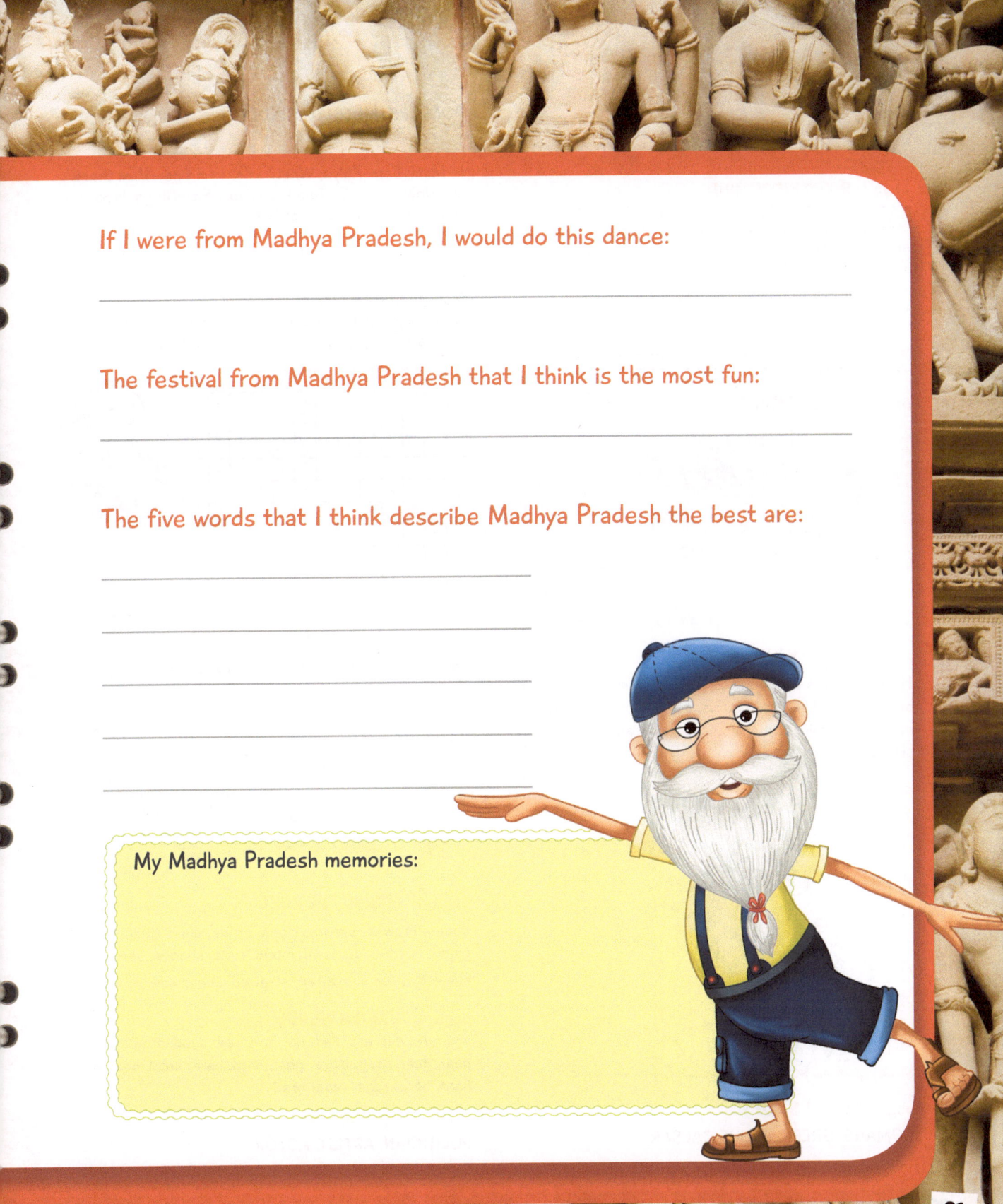

If I were from Madhya Pradesh, I would do this dance:

_____

The festival from Madhya Pradesh that I think is the most fun:

_____

The five words that I think describe Madhya Pradesh the best are:

_____

_____

_____

_____

_____

My Madhya Pradesh memories:

ANSWERS

page 9 RIVER WORD GRID

U	Y	N	R	E	W	Y	Q
U	Y	A	M	U	N	A	S
J	D	R	F	G	H	M	O
A	S	M	X	C	J	U	N
S	N	A	R	M	A	D	A
Z	A	D	S	V	W	A	N
Q	T	A	P	T	I	B	M
M	A	H	A	N	A	D	I

page 11 FOREST MAZE

page 13 HIDDEN WORDS

Here are some of the words you can form: air, ash, bag, ban, bar, big, bin, gas, has, his, nab, nib, rag, ran, rig, sir, bang, barn, gain, grab, hair, hang, rain, rang, rash, ribs, ring, sang, sing, snag

page 15 SPOT THE DIFFERENCE

page 17 WHAT'S ODD?

ROMANS, GREEK, JULIUS CAESAR

page 19 MIXED-UP WORDS

ROBBERS, MUGHAL, HINDI

page 21 LINGO SHINGO

I—Mein; Eat—Khiye; What?—Ka; I am fine—Hum theek ahi; How are you?—Tum kase aao?; Sit—Birajo; What are you doing?—Tum ka karat ho?

page 27 MATCH THEM RIGHT

Bhagoria—Put gulal and run; Tansen— A grand musical festival; Ijtima— One of the world's largest religious gatherings; Tertali—Carrying a sword between the teeth; Jawara—Carrying a basket of grain on their head

page 37 CROSSWORD TIME

page 39 RHYME TIME

court, port, sort, sport, thwart, tort, wart

page 41 HAPPY FARM

page 47 MISHKI THE POET

booed, brewed, brood, cooed, crude, cued, dude, feud, glued, hued, Jude, lewd, mood, rude, shooed, shrewd, skewed, slewed, stewed, strewed, sued, viewed, wooed

page 49 HIDDEN WORDS

age, are, ear, era, had, her, rag, red, aged, area, dare, dear, deer, drag, edge, gear, hard, hare, head, hear, heed, herd, here, rage, read, reed

page 53 ODD ONE OUT

POLITICIAN, ARTIST, ACTOR